"Lynda has created the blueprint for success in the wine hospitality industry. Everyone who works in a tasting room will benefit from reading this book!"
—Bill Adrian, Business Development, Clos Du Val Winery

"Our multi-bottle and case sales have increased 3-fold since the seminar— we definitely see a difference in our tasting room! Lynda's energy and confidence in sales is conveyed through her various examples and exercises. She really challenges you to examine your sales approach and hone the skills that are lacking at any sales level experience. These skills are not just about the sales delivery, but how to observe the non-verbal cues of a buyer. Her coaching also focuses on improving
the hospitality of a tasting room by creating a richer experience for the guest."
—Tracy Hart, Owner, Le Mulet Rouge Vineyard and Winery

"Your workshop was an unqualified success . . . sales and wine club conversion are high. If only we had done it sooner! Thanks for teaching us that "facts tell, stories sell."
—John Morris, Tasting Room Manager, Tablas Creek Vineyard

"We have seen great results . . . phenomenal! The staff is motivated and feels like they have the support, they are regularly helping each other out, and we could not be happier."
—Aaron Feaver, Tasting Room Manager,
Long Meadow Ranch Winery

"A go-to book for employees, reminding them of our unique and exciting job of selling wine. This back-pocket book should be in every tasting room break area for all to read and remain motivated. We are all so lucky to be in this business!"
—Christina Frakes, Hospitality Manager, St. Francis Winery

Romancing the
Grape

Romancing the *Grape*

Published by Success Strategies, Inc.
Library of Congress Cataloging-in-Publication Data is available on file.

Paperback ISBN: 978-0-9628039-0-1
E-book ISBN: 978-1-7327747-2-8

Cover and interior design: Jim Shubin, BookAlchemist.net

For special pricing for bulk purchases of the paperback book, contact SuccessStrategiesInc.com.

Romancing the
Grape

Relationship Selling
for Hospitality Professionals

Lynda R. Paulson

SUCCESS STRATEGIES, INC.

Acknowledgements

My heartfelt thanks to the following people who took the time to read the early manuscript, advise, correct, and encourage me along the way: Bill Adrian of Clos Du Val Winery; Nicole Cummings and Frank Nola of Cakebread Cellars; Bill Farmer of Raymond Winery; Christina Frakes of St. Francis Winery, and Victoria Adams of Casa Barranca Estate.

A special thanks to Karen Misuraca, my favorite wordsmith. Her belief in me and more help than you can imagine, and her expertise, meant everything to me.

CONTENTS

CHARDONNAY

Foreword

By Nicole Cummings, Cakebread Cellars

Vibrant, tenacious, vigorous, and charming—these are the characteristics of the wine blend that I would use to describe Lynda Paulson and her passion for Romancing the Grape. I met Lynda at a sales training she facilitated for our direct-to-consumer team. Little did I know that this enthusiastic and engaging trainer would captivate me by speaking a language that blended human and technical elements to build relationships and sell wine.

Her training revealed a new path that better connected us to our guests, a path that is all about developing lasting relationships with and creating remarkable experiences for our guests. This is the real competitive advantage for any winery or hospitality professional.

Understanding guests and customers goes beyond acknowledging the basic information required to be a competent professional. It is discovering the heart of who we are and the romance of the product we represent—our character and values, and the ability to relate to others. The more we know about ourselves and the values and purpose of our organizations, the better we connect with the guests and customers we serve.

The Greek teacher Socrates believed that the search for knowledge began with introspection: "know thyself." He believed his students should question themselves, and follow each question with another question, in a process called the Socratic Method. By following each question, they would come to realize that the answer lay within.

Some researchers refer to this search for self-knowledge as emotional intelligence, and some say that emotional intelligence is quantifiable. As the HR Director at Cakebread, I interview and hire employees with high emotional intelligence, and for good reason.

For wine hospitality and sales professionals, it is not enough to focus on acquiring self-knowledge. They must also know and effectively communicate grape varietal facts, growing regions, viticulture practices, winemaking styles and techniques, all while delivering extraordinary hospitality and appealing to each customer's needs and desires.

These opportunities and encounters demand that wine hospitality and sales professionals demonstrate mastery in both the technical and people relationship competencies that distinguish them. It is this integration that is portrayed in Lynda Paulson's book, and, it is this understanding that connected me to her unique and effective approach to Romancing the Grape!

PROLOGUE

In my more than thirty years of visiting and consulting with wineries, I have seen tremendous change. When I first moved to Napa, there was no charge to taste, you didn't need an appointment, and tourists wandered randomly from winery to winery.

Nowadays, even though wine tasting is more popular than ever, the guest experience is more programmed, more educational, and more rewarding for visitors. Tasting room personnel have evolved from servers to hospitality professionals and brand ambassadors. Appointments are often necessary, and food-and-wine pairings are offered. Winery hospitality is all about creating memorable occasions and welcoming visitors in to "join the family."

A handbook of tips and exercises and suggestions, this book will enhance your communication skills so that your guests will never forget their visit to your winery, and they won't leave the tasting room without purchasing wine! You are going to learn all about "relationship selling," which will come quite naturally to you once you understand the fundamentals. It's all about you as a unique, personable, enjoyable human being.

Nowadays as the industry has become so much more competitive, relationship selling "on the ground" at the winery is more important and more effective than ever. Social media, digital marketing, and DTC (Direct to Consumer) advertising, has transformed the connection to wine enthusiasts, getting right into their hearts and minds. We are impressed with Power Point presentations, ultra-professional websites, blogs and newsletters.

And yet, beyond all the commercial campaigns, you, as a warm and welcoming ambassador of your winery and its brand, are the main link between your visitors and the lifelong bond they could have, and should have, with your winery.

Personal relationships with customers have never been more important, and wineries are investing in them. Although a winemaker dinner is still a big deal, social, culinary and even cultural events at the wineries have become more creative and sophisticated. Club members are VIPs, enjoying private soirees in the owners' homes, cruises to Europe with winemakers, costume parties, and live music in the caves!

And yet, there is nothing quite like the one-on-one relationship that happens when a guest steps through the door into the tasting room, and the magic begins!

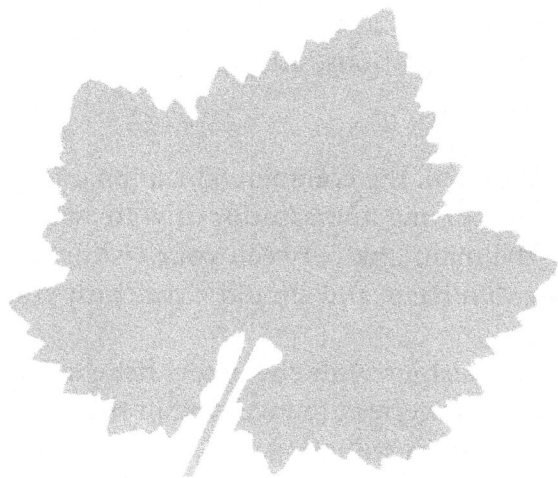

ZINFANDEL

Introduction

Having "mystery shopped" hundreds of wineries and talked to and observed their hospitality staff members, I know how challenging your job can be. You are at once a retail salesperson, a representative of the brand and the products of your winery, as well as the host of a party!

You were hired because your personality is well-suited to balancing all three of these job descriptions, and you are an outgoing "people person."

Wine Sales 101

Whether you have worked at a winery for years or if you are a newbie in the tasting room, this book will be either a motivating refresher course, or an introduction to the basics of wine sales and hospitality based on establishing personal relationships. You will find easy-to-use, enjoyable strategies that I have seen put into practice at wineries all over the country. I give you words and phrases to use, conversation openers, sales closers, greetings, approaches, questions and answers. You will find out what to do when your customers are out of sorts or distracted, and when they have had too much to drink.

In my winery sales and hospitality workshops, I have found that even the most experienced tasting room staff may lose touch with their primary purpose, which is to **build relationships and sell wine**. If that is not what you perceive as your primary purpose, take it from me, your employer does. In my workshops and in this book, I do not advocate or teach a hard-sell approach. I know that you want to be relaxed, confident and productive every day—and have some fun being with your visitors. After all, we're talking wine and the good life!

It's a Party!

You are presenting and selling a rather romantic, delicious, beautiful product that contributes greatly to people's lives and their special occasions, their vacations and parties, to milestones in their lives, and even to their personal and professional relationships.

People come to your winery to have a good time.

You are a host or hostess who puts on a party every day! Your guests come to taste and learn about wine, take some home to enjoy later, and discover the mystique and the legendary beauty of the Wine Country. Your task is to ensure that a good time is had by all, while encouraging visitors to buy wine, join the wine club, and always remember the good feeling they had at your winery.

> *The Tasting Room Manager at Raymond Vineyards, Bill Farmer said, "I am a stage manager. My job is to be here early to have everything set up so that our ambassadors can step onto their stage and immediately get into their role, which is to make our guests feel that they are the most important part of our day!"*

How to Use This Book

As a training professional for hundreds of wineries, I have found that everyone communicates and creates sales in different ways. For that reason, I encourage you to study this book as a basic manual of (proven) selling fundamentals, then, make it your own. Use a highlighter on those sections that really resonate with you! Make notes in the margins, and at the end of each chapter at "Your Thoughts," personalize how you will use my suggestions. And, do bring the book to work with you, for when you or your team could use some new ideas and reminders!

Relationship Selling

Your unique personality, wit and charm are what generate a natural flow of conversation with your guests and create personal relationships with them. The enjoyment they feel while at your tasting bar or table will translate into wine sales and into life-long memories of being at your winery.

With *Romancing the Grape*, you will learn how to create those relationships and sell wine in an easy-going, unpressured way, and have fun doing it!

One   First Impressions

You are the Message, the Star of the Show

It's showtime, baby! You are on stage. When someone comes through that door, look up, smile, and say something like, "Come on in!" Or, just say, "Welcome!" Then reach out to shake their hands, tell them your name and ask for theirs.

The first impression that you make to arriving guests establishes an immediate, welcoming atmosphere that encourages sales and positive, personal connections (if not, it may throw up a wall to the enjoyment of their visit).

You have greeted them, made eye contact, smiled, shaken hands with them, and you know their names;—believe me, your guests are already feeling really good about being there. When you let guests see and feel how much you love being a winery host and making them feel important and comfortable, you are off to the best possible start.

The first contact—make it positive and memorable.

If that magic dust doesn't sparkle the moment someone enters your tasting room, your visitors may wander around on their own and eventually belly up to the tasting bar, and yet, the chances that you'll sell them wine have already diminished.

> *My sister-in-law and her daughter wandered into one of the longest established, most renowned wineries in Sonoma, wearing shorts and running shoes. The two women stood behind a group at the tasting bar. Staff members looked up, apparently assumed that the casually dressed women were unimportant, and looked away. Feeling unwelcome, the two walked downtown into another tasting room where they were warmly welcomed, and they hung out for an hour or so before choosing several wines to take home.*

Greet Every Guest, Every Time

Remember that you "own" the environment and you create the atmosphere. Over several decades, I have conducted hundreds of mystery shopping assignments. Posing as prospective customers who are exhibiting obvious buying signals, my companions and I continue to be amazed that we are greeted less than half of the time. As we taste wine, seldom do the employees notice or respond to our buying signals, such as, "Which one shall we buy? I love this wine! Wouldn't this be great for the party?"

> *Sometimes I wonder if the barrier of reserve*
> *and hesitation that surrounds customers*
> *also surrounds tasting room hosts.*

Making the Connection

Acknowledge each individual as soon as you can, especially those who have been waiting, just as you would in your home. Simple friendliness, a smile and eye contact go a long, long way. Many of your guests are from out of state and/or from other countries, and they may feel intimidated by the elegant ambiance of your winery, or unsure of what to expect in a tasting room. It's your job to put their minds at ease and to prepare them for an exceptional experience.

> *Shannon Muracchioli of Clos du Val said, "I have always encouraged the team to consider the efforts that each visitor may have taken to walk through our doors. Did they take their previous vacation time, save for months, arrange care for their children and their pets, all to get to this place? We can ensure that each welcome is what it should be."*

The impressions and the memories that you create for a guest may be not only the highlight of their day, but the highlight of their entire visit to the Wine Country. Think of ways to establish an atmosphere of welcome and fun—after all, wine is a part of a fabulous lifestyle!

On one of my mystery shopping expeditions in New York state, where wineries are scattered rather widely apart in beautiful, rolling countryside, my companions and I drove into a parking lot, and as we got out of the car, a smiling person walked out of the winery, waited for us to approach and said, "Welcome everyone, come right on in." Surprised, we immediately felt like VIPs, and we spent money there that day, just like VIPs.

Those who sell the most wine in tasting rooms are highly motivated, high-energy, people-loving communicators. They know that creating personal relationships with customers results in higher, more predictable sales. Some people call it relationship selling, some call it consultative selling. I call it making the connection.

For many people, the visit to your part of the country and to your winery may, in fact, be once in a lifetime.

Selling isn't about persuasion, it's about what emerges naturally from you when you show genuine interest in your guests and express a desire to help them have a great experience at your winery. Your smile, your friendliness and the personal connections you make are what make up your "like factor." People will like and remember you if you are warm and approachable, and come across as happy with yourself and your job.

Some of us like to entertain, use humor, tell stories. Others are more low-key and like to focus on the wine. Just be your natural self and your guests will feel comfortable.

**People may not remember the wine they drank
or even your name,
but they will remember how you made them feel.**

Customers are apt to enjoy their visit and buy wine when they sense that their guide or host is interested in them and likes them as individuals. The way you show interest is to find out who they are.

The tasting room manager at Roblar Winery in Santa Barbara County, Brian York, said, "When a customer comes to the winery, I try and identify their specific needs. I also pay attention to what they look like and what their interests are. Greeting the customer by name, every single time they arrive at the winery, makes them feel appreciated, as if they are there for a very important reason."

Asking the Right Questions

The most successful salespeople are avid listeners. The more closely they listen, the sooner they get to know their customers, and the better they can personalize an approach that results in sales, or at the very least, in a memorable experience for their guests.

Listening to and getting to know your visitors comes across as expressing genuine interest, and that is the magic touch.

To find out a few basics about your guests, ask questions, then let them talk. People like to talk about themselves, and the more you subtly encourage them to do that, the more comfortable they will be. Listening also helps you "read" your guests, and gives you visual clues as to who they are and their state of mind. Start out by asking, "Of all the wineries in the valley, how did you choose ours? This should be one of the very first questions you ask, because it almost always opens up a world of information that will start your relationship and give you an idea of how to proceed.

Here are a few more questions to get the conversation going:

> What brings you to the Napa/Sonoma/Temecula valley?
>
> You look like pros on the winery circuit. How can I help you today?
>
> What other wineries have you visited?
>
> Where are you from? Where are you staying?
>
> You all seem to be having a good time. How long will you be here in Carmel Valley?
>
> What have you been doing for fun?
>
> What's the weather like back home in Fargo?

Have a few questions or topics ready that you can pull out when you are not sure what to say, or when you feel less than gregarious. If you can't think of anything to ask, offer a few compliments:

That is a great hat. Did you get that here in the Willamette Valley?

I am admiring your earrings . . your glasses . . that lovely bracelet

Is your dog (or your baby . . .) always so good?

Getting to Know You

Every question you ask makes your visitors believe that you are interested in them. You are not interrogating, you are getting to know them and helping them choose wines that they may not have discovered on their own. Asking questions is how you create a warm, friendly and helpful atmosphere and that "once-in-a-lifetime" feeling that people will remember.

What do you like to drink at home?

What do you look for on a wine list? Red, white, sparkling?

How often do you serve wine?

Do you collect wine?

Tell me where you usually buy wine?

Did you happen to see the Wine Spectator review of this one?

> *When I asked one hospitality host where I could buy their premium wines (a huge buying signal), instead of saying "right here at the winery" or "at finer wine shops," he told me that the best place to buy their wines is Costco or Trader Joe's. SERIOUSLY?*

When visitors seem a little tentative about what to do or say, encourage them by offering a few options. At Tablas Creek Winery in Paso Robles, they have a lovely way of asking, "What would you like to know?" Try questions like these:

Tell me what you are most interested in today?

Shall we start with the whites or go right into the reds?

Would you like to see the cellar? the vineyard? the bottling line?

Do you want to learn more about winemaking?

Would you like to hear about what makes our winery different from the others you've been to?

Are you planning to take some wine home to add to your wine collection?

YOUR THOUGHTS

What questions could you ask
to encourage conversation with your guests?

_____

_____

_____

_____

_____

_____

_____

_____

_____

_____

TWO   Personality and Body Language: Programming for Success

We all like happy, positive, upbeat people who make us feel good and put us at ease. You have no control over who wanders into your tasting room, but you can decide, in advance, how you will create a warm, welcoming experience for them, no matter who they are, and how you will sell them some wine!

By practicing a few mind-training techniques, you can improve and even transform your demeanor. Remember that people see, hear and feel your attitude. Soften your natural reserve by opening up a bit and learning to self-talk. Try these positive affirmations by saying to yourself:

> I love people and they love my enthusiasm.
> I am organized, prepared, and looking forward to this day.
> I am good at this. I love what I do.
> I express confidence and warmth toward my guests.
> Our visitors are drawn to me. They like to hear what I have
>   to say.
> I enjoy helping people select wine they will love.

By programming your subconscious mind, you can increase your sales, have more fun at work and create a turning point in your life! You can't buy a good attitude, you have to work at it! You'll find that the more you work at it, the better you become.

Enthusiasm Sells

Just being nice is hardly enough in today's competitive sales environment. Prospective customers can buy good wine in a zillion places other than your winery.
Don't just sell the wine—sell yourself!

Francis Ford Coppola Winery (yes, that FF Coppola) in the Sonoma County Wine Country is one of my favorite places to take friends, because the hospitality staffers there are about the most enthusiastic greeters and hosts I've ever come across. The Hospitality Training and Development Manager, James Luchini, told me, "The Coppola family promises to make every visit to the winery memorable and unique," and they do. At the tasting bars, in a lively, fun way, they present the facts and benefits of their wines along with personal anecdotes of what goes on around the winery, and of course, stories about their boss, the famous movie director.

Browsing through the employment section of the Coppola website, I found some enlightening content:

> *"Ours is a high-energy, professional workplace where we offer outstanding customer service, and have fun along the way." "(We hire) energetic and enthusiastic people who provide exceptional customer service to guests, enhance company image, and facilitate communication to guests."*

Your Body Talks

The combination of how you stand and move, your appearance and how you use your voice all create a dramatic image of who you are and how others perceive you. You send messages with your posture, tone of voice and speed of speech. Even your hair creates a barrier if it shields some of your face.

> *It is said that 85% of communication is non-verbal.*

Do some people-watching to see what I mean. Do some people have a closed-up look with hands and arms, and sometimes legs and feet, clasped together, close to the body?

Do their heads tilt down or away, with eyes downcast? Are their voices a low mumble? Do you get the idea that they want to avoid human contact at all costs? With whom would you like to have a conversation?

General aspects of body language involve open vs. closed demeanor. People perceived to be friendly, approachable, trustworthy, relaxed and confident have an erect posture with hands and arms open, head tilted toward their customer, and direct, but undemanding, eye contact. And, they are smiling!

Ever notice what happens to our eyebrows when you smile? Look in the mirror and smile. Your eyebrows naturally go up. Put on a neutral expression and your eyebrows drop. With your eyebrows up, say, "I had a wonderful time!" Now, with a neutral face, say, "I had a wonderful time." Hear the difference?

Watch facial expression in TV ads and YouTube videos. If they want you to buy something, they smile with an open face and raised eyebrows.

Physically, what can you do to expand and enhance your presence and hold the attention of your visitor? To establish trust and friendliness so that people feel comfortable enough to buy from you, think LARGE with your physical gestures. Make the most of your space behind the bar by moving around, thereby expressing kinetic energy and enthusiasm. Project your expertise and your confidence by standing up straight and speaking up clearly.

Avoid "preening" moves, such as brushing your hair back with your hands, rubbing your face or adjusting your clothes. Do not tug on your ear, rock back and forth, play with your buttons or your rings. Fidgeting and nervous movements make other people nervous, too, and cancel out the relaxed atmosphere that you are trying to create.

Rather than wait for guests to come to you, whenever you can possibly manage to do this, come out from behind your tasting bar to greet visitors and shake their hands. You would be surprised how seldom this happens at hospitality venues. Warmth and sincerity is easily transmitted by that handshake. (Pats and hugs are out unless you know your guests very well.)

Listen to Yourself

Speak in front of a mirror and notice how the expression on your face affects your voice. In addition to the warmth or the impassiveness that your face imparts, your voice tells the listener a lot about you, about your age, your gender and education level, and certainly about your attitude and level of confidence.

When you have a chance to listen to and watch yourself in a video, that can be enlightening. Try practicing your greeting, your "soft" sales pitches, and your guided tour by videoing yourself with your smartphone. Do you come across as lively and interested, or slow, bored or even silly? Do you speak every word clearly, or do you mutter and drop your voice? Women's voices often get higher and higher, while men's voice drop lower and lower, making it difficult for people to understand them.

If you have a low-energy voice or if you speak too fast, practice slowing your pace while enlivening your tone. Tune in to Martha Stewart's YouTube channel to watch and listen to how she speaks so clearly and slowly, yet how friendly and conversational she seems.

YOUR THOUGHTS

When you're feeling a little low,
what do you say to yourself to raise your spirits?

_____

_____

_____

What are some of your personal and unique presentation and
communication assets? List as many as you can. If you're not
sure, ask a friend to describe your strengths.

_____

_____

_____

In what areas could you improve?

_____

_____

_____

THREE Romancing the Grape

Stories that Sell

> *At a winery in New York state, I learned about and tasted ice wine, the sweet, after-dinner concoction that is uncommon, and often unavailable, in the West where I live. When I purchased a bottle, the tasting room host cradled it in her hands, and said, "I'm going to package this carefully for your flight, and when you get home, put it away in a cool place. When you have a special evening coming up, chill the bottle and two glasses, and when the moment is right, bring it out and tell your husband that you have something special for him. Tell him that this is the nectar of the gods, a sweet, sexy potion that will change his life."*

Well, I did exactly as she told me to do, and my husband and I will never forget that winery (or that evening). I have since purchased the wine online and recommended that label many times to friends.

Your visitors are imagining a certain romantic lifestyle that is achieved, in part, by the wine that they enjoy at home, in restaurants, and when offering to friends. By focusing on the magic and the romance of wine,
you are helping make their dreams come true.

Consider adding a few real-life anecdotes to your tasting room presentation and/or winery tours. Describe a surprising vertical tasting that you attended, or the time you met an icon of the industry, or served a great wine at a family reunion. People will remember your stories long after they've forgotten about malolactic fermentation.

Another way to romance the wine and the winery is to tell little stories about the family who owns the winery or about the winemaker. Of all the facts and benefits and everything else that you relate to your guests, it's the stories they will remember.

> *I recall an enjoyable tour led by Robert Owings at Del Dotto Vineyards. Wine is what we came for and that's what he gave us as soon as we arrived, handing us each a glass of wine. He then spun a tale of how his employer, a former TV host, got into the wine business. Spit buckets and water were stationed throughout the winery, so that we could clear our palates for tasting more wines as we cruised along. By the time we got back to the tasting bar, we were in love with the wine and the winery, and we bought several bottles.*

Words that Sell, Evoke and Enhance

**Brain scans reveal that when people hear words
that are evocative or emotional,
different areas of their brain are stimulated.**

Using a vivid vocabulary as you serve wine is a powerful stimulant of the sensory cortex. Try it! Instead of the usual words like apricot, grassy, chocolatey and the like, experiment with using words like luscious, sexy, and juicy.

What new words and phrases would evoke the sensory qualities of your wonderful wines?

Legendary, rare, masterpiece

Luscious, ripe, voluptuous, sumptuous

Smooth, subtle, sophisticated

Juicy, fruity, ambrosial, creamy

For lovers, velvety, black tie

The Audrey Hepburn of Pinot!

Dense, dark, intense

Earthy, hearty, rustic, zesty, bold

Clean, fresh, green, crisp, refreshing

As sexy as Lady Gaga!

Aromatic, fragrant, bouquet

Award-winning, highly-rated, medal-winning

Exclusive, the Rolls-Royce of Cabernets

White House worthy

Beautiful Bouquets

Come up with ways to describe the tantalizing aromas of your wines. Motivate and energize your customers by spending a minute or two teaching them about the bouquets—how and why to take deep inhalations before tasting, and letting the wine rest on the tongue. (Is it okay to taste the wine yourself along with your guests? Maybe, maybe not. Be sure to check with your employer about their policy on this important issue.)

Make the tasting experience interactive by involving your guests as you go along, asking:

How would you describe this Pinot?

Have you ever tasted a Sangiovese like this one?

How do you like the blend?
Have you found a favorite?
How do you like that finish?
What "yum factor" do you give this one?

YOUR THOUGHTS

What evocative vocabulary can you add to your presentations?
Choose at least one NEW word for each wine you pour.

Wine: _____

New Word: _____

Wine: _____

New Word: _____

Wine: _____

New Word:_____

Wine: _____

New Word: _____

Wine:_____

New Word: _____

FOUR   Facts, Benefits and Bridges

People buy warm benefits, before they buy cold facts. They don't buy things and they don't buy information—they buy wants, needs and dreams. They buy what something will do for them and how it will make them feel. Above all, you are selling enjoyment, enhancement of a lifestyle, and in the case of cult wines, status. Sell the pleasure, sell the fun!

Facts may be the soil, the growing region, the history of the winery, the oak or stainless-steel barrels, and the details of this year's harvest. Benefits? They may be the unique blend, the cherry-chocolate finish, the winemaker's legendary style, and the reputation of the name on the label.

People buy benefits, not facts.
What are the benefits of your wines?

It has been my experience that many winery tour guides have a spiel all about the process of winemaking, the locations of the vineyards, the definition of malolactic fermentation, the size of the barrels and what they cost, the number of months in the barrel, the temperature in the cellar, the year the winery opened, the number of cases produced . . . facts, numbers, wine terms. How much is too much?

People unfamiliar with winemaking may find all of this fascinating, if—a big if—the presentation of facts is balanced with benefits to them as individuals. Try to find out how much they already know before your launch into your talk, and excite your guests with your information, rather than boring or exhausting them. Use just two or three descriptors about each wine.

As educators and ambassadors of your brand, you deliver your winery's story, history, and the facts about the wines. While your guests appreciate your expertise, I suggest that you give them more by bridging facts with benefits.

Here are typical facts and phrases I have heard from hospitality teams over the years:

Cool evenings and sunny days

Two years in sweet French oak, stainless steel tanks

Hand-crafted

Volcanic-based, gravelly soil

Planted low to the ground

Planted in tight rows

Extra-long hang-time

Youthful vines, old vines

2-2.5 tons per acre

Organic, biodynamic

Gravity flow architecture

Dry farming

Sound familiar?

Now, review this list and add other facts that you usually mention, then add a benefit to each fact. For example:

Cool evenings and sunny days = produce an expressive, aromatic and complex wine. Luscious and refreshing!

Two years in sweet French oak = bring out a flamboyant and intense black cherry concentration and velvety smooth tannins.

**Changes or additions to long-established habits are best remembered when done in small increments.
Be patient with yourself
as you add new ideas to your presentations.**

Bridges

A secret of sales professionals: they use bridges to connect facts with benefits. Always connect a fact to each benefit that you mention, using phases like this:

> "Which means" or "Which means to you"
> "You will like (love) that because"
> "I tell you that because"
> "Our winemaker does that because"
> "That is significant because"

Why use a bridge? Like using a yellow highlighter in a book, a bridge highlights the fact and relates it to real life. Notice the use of "you" in the bridge, which creates a psychological connection, making it more personal.

You can even fact/bridge/benefit the price of your wine! I have seen and heard this bridge used to great success. Not at all a hard sell, it stresses scarcity and appeals to discerning buyers.

> *Fact*: this red blend is our signature wine. It is $125. ($250, $450, etc.)
> *Bridge*: the significance of this price is . . .
> *Benefit*: we produce just a few cases of this extraordinary wine, and the availability is limited to one bottle (case) per person.

Here are a few more examples of turning facts into benefits by using bridges.

> *Fact:* the grapes in this wine are from a rocky hillside at 2,000 feet, where they are influenced by cool evenings and the harsh limestone soil.
> *Bridge:* which means you will enjoy
> *Benefit:* a complex, refined, deeply aromatic Cabernet redolent of black currant, chocolate and cassis.
>
> *Fact:* this vineyard-designated blend of Malbec and Syrah comes from the dry, sunny appellation in the Lodi area.
> *Bridge:* you will appreciate that because
> *Benefit:* this hearty, fruit-forward red wine is dense and hearty, making it perfect for spicy foods.
>
> *Fact:* this Bordeaux-style wine is a blend of Cabernet Sauvignon and Cabernet Franc, aged two years in French oak.
> *Bridge:* I mention that because
> *Benefit:* the result is an intense, black cherry flavor with velvety smooth tannins.

Nail Downs

Nail downs are wonderful tools that help you recognize where guests are in their interest level, and their readiness to buy, and they also help you to stop talking and get them to talk!

It is so important to take the time for a two-way conversation, rather than just you doing all the talking. The nail down is a question that comes after the benefit, and it sounds like this:

> Is that something you like in a red blend?
>
> Is that a style you like to serve . . . to drink?
>
> Would that be important to you?
>
> Do you like that style of Sauvignon Blanc?

After the nail down, stop talking and wait until they respond. You will then learn where your guests are in your presentation, and in the personal relationship you are attempting to create. They will say things like, "This is wonderful . . . perfect . . . great for my mom, or our party or the dog sitter."

Or, they may say they really do not like it, and they may not pay attention to you, avoiding response and eye contact. All

49

of these responses tell you where you are with them, and how to proceed.

Remember, your purpose is to connect with people, not to lecture them.

Take the time to pause and allow guests to ask questions and make comments—this is supposed to be relaxing! Here are ways to clarity as you present your benefits.

I point that out to show you that . . .

We take the time with the winemaking process so that . . .

When you open this Merlot, you will appreciate the fact that . . .

Have you ever opened a wine and noticed a musty smell? We avoid that altogether by . . .

This Sauvignon Blanc is affordable, so it's great for parties.

If you have asked a few questions of your guests and found out a little about their lives, you can then relate the qualities (benefits) of some of your wines to their lifestyle or their part of the country. If they are from Texas and like to barbecue, point out how well your hearty Burgundies stand up to the intense flavors of beef and Southwestern cuisine. If your visitors are on anniversary, honeymoon or birthday trips, talk about sparkling wine or varietals that go with fancy desserts and special occasions.

> European wines can be quite different from American wines, so you might ask your Spanish, German and French visitors what they enjoy in their part of the world. Rather than treating every group of wine tasters the same, making personal connections in this way shows real thoughtfulness on your part.

Stand Out in Your Field

Make your sales presentations memorable by describing what makes your winery different from all the rest. Of all of the Cabs produced in the Napa Valley, what distinguishes yours? Why are your Italian varietals award-winners? What makes your Pinot Grigios sell out every year?

Backed by your knowledge of what your competition is offering, bring your products to life and importance by comparing your wines with those of other wineries (you don't have to name them). Answer this question: Why should I buy your Zinfandel or your Cabernet or Merlot instead of those down the road?

When mystery shopping, I often ask, "What are you famous for? or, best known for?"

Your ability to set your wines and your winery apart from all the others is one of the best ways to show benefits. If you are not sure what distinguishes your winery and your wines, **I suggest that you get some input from your winemaker, and occasionally go on tasting expeditions to other wineries.** You may pick up some new tricks of the trade, and you will develop a much better idea of how your wines and your hospitality experience compare to the rest.

You will find that each hospitality experience, tasting room and tour is different in attitude and ambiance created by the staff and the property itself. As the ambassador of your brand and the "wine whisperer" of your wonderful products, to the guest in the tasting room, you are the number one creator of what makes your winery unique.

Food, Wine and the Seasons

Food and wine are meant for each other. Pairing food with wine is part of the romance and the benefits, and it's certainly a major reason why people buy and drink wine. If visitors are spending a day, a weekend or a vacation in your area (and you'll know because you asked), you already know they have food and restaurants on their minds.

Food and wine pairing can be complicated and intimidating for some people, so your suggestions are very welcome. Encourage a sale by mentioning that your full-bodied Zinfandel goes very well with spicy foods, or that your flowery, lemony Sauvignon Blanc is perfect with seafood and salads. Offer seasonal pairing ideas, such as Rosé for Thanksgiving dinner or a grassy picnic wine in the summertime.

> Hearty varietals for BBQ
> What goes with spicy Mexican and Italian food?
> How about Cabs and Syrahs for winter stews?
> Sparkling wines with appetizers and desserts
> Pairing red wines with chocolate
> Lighter varietals with seafood

Corkage can be a sales tool. You might let your visitors know which restaurants in your area do not charge corkage—there are usually a few—and suggest a few of your wines to go with those menus. Also, you can suggest that they bring home a few bottles for a blind tasting or a vertical tasting for their friends.

In the Buying Mood

They are in the mood! At no time are customers more open to buy than when they have already committed to a purchase.

Make a few suggestions:

> Shall we fill up this six-bottle box?
> By buying two bottles today or joining our wine club, we can waive the tasting fee (only if management agrees; not all wineries offer this).
> How about one to enjoy right away and two to lay down?
> Only one? (only two?)
> You might want to take advantage of the case discount.
> Before we ring this up, would you like some time to browse in the gift shop? Check out the Reidel glassware, the Italian pottery, the . . . .
> How about a couple extra for gifts?

Did you see those beautiful bottle bags?
You just bought one of my two most favorite wines. (Wine tasters always want to know about your favorites. This one works every time!)

> *While mystery shopping at a winery, although I stood at the tasting bar raving about their Sauvignon Blanc (one of my favorite wines), I just wasn't getting a "close" from the tasting room host. I usually leave without making a purchase unless I'm encouraged to buy, but in this case, I really wanted my Sauvignon Blanc, so I said I would buy a bottle. In a flash of genius, the host said, "Only one?"*

What a great "add-on! (I bought six...)

YOUR THOUGHTS

Which benefit and bridge phrases would you be most comfortable using with your guests?

Which "nail-down" and "add-on" questions will you experiment with?

_____

_____

_____

_____

_____

_____

_____

FIVE   Buying Signals

Your customer is telling you something and if you pay attention, you will see and hear it. A buying signal is something a person says or does when they are visualizing themselves enjoying, giving, purchasing and/or drinking your wine, whether on that very day or at home or for a gift. If you look for them, you will recognize some of the typical "I'm ready to buy" signals.

> Making notes on the wine menu, asking for the library wine menu.
>
> Looking at the label or the item more closely.
>
> Showing the wine to their companion(s), discussing it with them.
>
> Checking the wallet.
>
> Nodding the head and giving prolonged eye contact.
>
> Walking around with a bottle or an item from the gift shop in their hands.
>
> Scratching the head or the chin.

> *The tasting room menu is a powerful sales tool. Make sure it's paper, not laminated, and hand your guests pens or pencils.*
> *Encourage them to make notes*
> *and check off the wines they loved the most.*

A ready buyer may say:

> How much is this? Is there a quantity discount?
> Do you take American Express? Out of state checks?
> What could I serve with this?
> How can I get this home?
> My husband is a Zinfandel lover!
> Can I get this in half bottles? Can I get a discount on a
>   mixed case?
> How much do I need for 50 people?
> May I have another taste of the Merlot?
> We should take some home to your mother (or to
>   the babysitter!).
> My wife (husband) will kill me! (that means, they just
>   bought it . . .)

People do not like to be sold, but they love to buy!

Close the Sale with Conversation

You have greeted your customers, made eye contact, listened, asked the right questions, created a friendly atmosphere, guided them around the winery. You've expounded on the glories of your wines and watched for buying signals—and now, it's time to close the sale!

When my shopping partners and I mystery shop at a winery, one of us assumes the role of the buyer and the other is her cheerleader, encouraging her to buy. We come prepared to actually buy wine and we agree in advance that we will not buy unless we are "closed." I might say, "I love this. It's absolutely perfect for the party we're having." Or, "Merlot is my favorite. I always serve it with Mexican food."

After presenting all kinds of buying signals, from raving about the wine to asking about shipping, gift wrapping, discounts and the like, we wait for the close, and it usually doesn't come, so we don't buy. Even after all these years of mystery shopping wineries, we are always amazed when our obvious buying signals are ignored. Try mystery shopping yourself at other wineries and you'll see what I mean.

Of course, you would never be a pushy salesperson or strong-arm your guests into a purchase; that would erase all the rapport and connection that you have so carefully created. Nonetheless, you CAN sell wine to most of your guests if you focus on it, and, why wouldn't you? Nudging people to buy your wine is doing them a big favor—you know they'll love it.

Visualize each visitor walking out of your tasting room with at least one bottle of your wine, and visualize them joining your wine club!

Challenge yourself to make the sale. By now, your guests know you care about them and they've learned what your wine will contribute to their lives. Practice these various types of closes to gently direct your guests towards a purchase.

Trial Close

This is a soft close, because you're asking for an opinion, not a decision. For instance, when someone is browsing through your wine club brochure, a trial close would be: "If you were to join the club, which level would be best for you?"

When you ask for an opinion, you will get an answer, and thereby find out where they are in the relationship you are creating.

Direct Close

How many would you like?

What would you like to take home?

So, this is the one?

I see by your notes that you've made some choices.

Would you like to take that with you or shall we deliver it
to your hotel?

May I make a suggestion?

Shall I have our winemaker sign a few bottles for you?

(Big smile . .) Have you decided?

Visionary Close

Visualize the look on their faces when you serve this!

Can you just **imagine** how that will go with fish. . . Italian
food . . steak?

Just **picture** this sparkling wine at your party, the wedding.

Your family will love you for bringing the sparkling wine to
the anniversary (birthday) party!

Your friends at home are probably dying to try some of
the wine that you bring back from this trip! Imagine their
reaction when you pour this Petite Syrah!

Recommendation Close

This type of close is used by professional consultants and is based on the presumed authority of the presenter—you are the authority!

> Based on what you like to cook, I suggest . . .
>
> Based on what you've said so far, I recommend . . .
>
> For your hot summers in Texas, this Sauvignon Blanc would be refreshing.
>
> Shall I find out and let you know where you can buy this in Atlanta?
>
> Thinking about your party coming up, your best bet would be . . .

Assumptive Close

A great example of this close is when a man goes to Nordstrom's for a shirt, and the salesperson deftly shows him a matching tie, and a belt, and perhaps a sweater. That's building a relationship that results in brand loyalty and repeat sales.

So, is that the one?

You just picked one of my all-time favorite wines!

You have made some great choices. Shall we fill this six-bottle box?

Shall we add two more to fill the case?

So, the estate Cabernet and the proprietary blend are the ones?

Reminder Close

Remember, the Chardonnay you love is available only here at the winery.

This is a rare Cab that you won't find on many wine lists.

You can always call me and I'll ship that fabulous Cabernet to you before Christmas.

One last note about encouraging sales: let your voice help you become an effective closer—soft, friendly, caring, not pushy or aggressive. Speaking slowly, don't rush or come across as hurried or impatient. Concentrate on those buying signals and respond to them as if you are leading your customers gently by the arm.

Acknowledge Every Sale

Don't fail to reaffirm every sale, every time, by saying something like: *"You are going to love opening that Pinot Noir at home, and remembering your trip to Oregon."*

Always make your guests feel good about the buying decisions they make. *"I'm so happy you chose the sparkling wine!"*

YOUR THOUGHTS

What buying signals have you seen or heard recently?
Think outside the winery, too.

_____

_____

_____

_____

_____

What would you feel comfortable doing or saying when you see or hear a buying signal?

_____

_____

_____

_____

Which closes would you be most comfortable using? What words and phrases would you use?

_____

_____

_____

_____

SIX   Creative Selling, Add-ons, Phone Sales

Where is the Gift Shop?

Many wineries invest time, money and marketing consultation on displaying merchandise within or near their tasting rooms. Often, the items are high-end and made especially for the winery. No once, NOT ONCE, in a tasting room has anyone suggested that I browse in the gift shop area, and not once have tasting bar hosts mentioned merchandise.

When guests are encouraged to wander around in the retail area, chances are they will buy accessories or logo items. Don't you want them to go home with your winery's logo on their baseball cap?

High-ticket items are the easiest to add on.

Once your customer has purchased or intends to purchase several hundred dollars' worth of wine, he or she is a prime candidate for adding gifts and wine accessories—all you have to do is walk them over to the shop! Don't be shy about this. Think of selling related items as a special service.

Your guests are customers, and they love to purchase souvenirs of their visits and gifts to bring home. Don't miss out on these add-on and creative selling opportunities.

> *Why are your guests not directed to the shop?*
> *I believe it is because:*
>
> • *You may be unfamiliar with the merchandise."*
>
> • *You are not sure how to make the suggestion without seeming pushy.*
>
> • *It is thought of as a self-serve area.*

Here are some conversational ways to suggest that, after making their wine choices, that your guests browse in the winery shop.

Walk up to guest with a big smile and say something like, "I see you are looking at our Pinot Noir glassware. These are made by Reidel, the best glassmaker in the business. Are you familiar with that company"?

"Did you know that those purses are made of cork? They are unique, aren't they? What a great gift for your friends at home."

"How do you like the design on that china? They are made in Italy. How do you like that type of art"?

Three comfortable phrases to get it started:

- I see you are looking at _____?
- Did you know that _____?
- How do you like _____?

When your greeting or approach ends with a question, that asks for a response, and a nice conversation is started.

To make the most of your gift shop sales challenge, get to know the merchandise. Try to spend a few minutes every day looking at the gift and souvenir items and coming up with a knowledgeable tidbit about each one. Your retail sales clerk in the shop should be able to help you with this. Trust me, when you make add-on sales, that speaks volumes about your willingness to go the extra mile for your employers. You will be the hospitality host who really performs.

Phone Sales

Unless you are on video phone set-up, your obvious communication tool when connecting by phone, is the sound and the "personality" of your voice. People can hear your attitude, your confidence, your friendliness, your knowledge and your disposition, just by listening to you.

Tune Up Your Voice

Here are a few suggestions to make the very best of the phone communication relationship.

Smile: Make your phone calls in front of a mirror. You will soon see how your voice changes when you smile! Also, raise your eyebrows to create a positive, upbeat voice.

Move Around: If at all possible, walk around while you talk, or if you can't walk, try standing. You'll find that gesturing and speaking with enthusiasm and vitality results in a fresh dimension of physical and emotional energy. You will come across as invested in your listener, conversational, and happy to be connecting with them.

Match Their Style: Whether your customer is low-key, robust, playful or thoughtful, match their pace and tone; try not to be lower or higher than they are.

Use a Check List: Outline your talking points, and keep your plan simple, so you remain spontaneous.

Chat: Having a real conversation is a great opportunity to build the relationship. Take advantage of their openness!

**Take breaks from your phone calls.
Walk around, stretch, and focus on other things for ten minutes.**

Access Their History: If available in advance, check your customer's buying and event history with the winery. If you do not have their history, ask them, and make notes.

More Conversation

Keep the conversation going by mentioning the latest news about the wines or winery events, and be prepared with knowledge and details when they have questions. Use non-confrontative lead-ins and soft-selling phrases like these:

> *"Did you know* about our new release of your favorite varietals?
>
> *"Let me tell you* about something exciting (new) we are doing!
>
> *"You might want to* consider a case. Shipping is discounted this month.

How you make your customers feel with this phone call will give you the result you are hoping for. Remember . . . *you are the winery!*

YOUR THOUGHTS

What are your favorite items in the gift shop? How do you describe them?

_____

_____

_____

_____

How might you suggest to your guests that they stop in at the retail area?

_____

_____

_____

_____

What are you phone communication strengths?
How can you improve them to make more sales?

_____

_____

_____

_____

_____

_____

SEVEN
Busy Weekends and Special Events
Big Groups

Hosting a lot of people at the same time takes talent and a unique set of skills. Whether a winemaker dinner, a large seated tasting, or a big group at the bar, it can be challenging. This is the time to strut your stuff, and to become physically and vocally more impressive, resulting in a more compelling connection and positive attention from your audiences.

Even when you are swamped with crowds of people who all come in at the same time, try your darndest to smile and make eye contact with as many as possible, even if just for a few seconds. This is a very special "showtime" occasion, and you need to use your big positive attitude!

At the Tasting Bar

When dealing with several small groups or one big group, put up your forefinger and say, "Come right over here, we'll be right with you!" Research shows that if spoken to or acknowledged in some way, most customers will wait up to

twenty-five minutes to be accommodated (as long as they have
a glass of wine . . .).

> *At one winery we visited, they run a group through
> every thirty minutes. We were five minutes late, and
> the man who checked us in was frustrated with us
> and his job in general. Rather unfriendly, he came
> across as just doing his job. This was not a pleasant
> start to our day of wine tasting.*

Especially when you are short-handed, keep moving and keep
smiling! At Ponte Vineyard in Temecula, I watched a young
host work miracles behind the long, long tasting bar that was
packed with guests. She strolled up and down, pausing briefly
at each guest, saying, "Are you ready for more? How about a
splash of that amazing Zinfandel? You're next, what can I
pour for you? What would you like to take home with you
today?"

All by herself in a room full of visitors, she smiled, poured, talked up the wine, and engaged with her guests like this:

> Tell me what you want (need, like).
>
> Let me know if you would like a second taste of that Cabernet.
>
> Let me know when you decide on some wine to take home.
>
> Just wave when you are ready for the next taste.

As you keep moving, closing sales at a moment's notice, your guests can see that you are busy and taking care of everyone as pleasantly as possible. Keep up that positive, friendly attitude, and thank them for their patience. Be upbeat, make it fun, and remember, it's a party, and it's "showtime!"

When it gets really busy, try one or two of these statements:

> We're setting up for you right now. Please make yourselves comfortable.
> Would you mind if I left you for a moment?
> I'll be right back

Please enjoy the wine for another moment, and I'll get
    back to you.
Don't let us ignore you!
Let me know if you have questions.
(And the magic words, with a smile) I'll be right with you!

Bring in the Expert: Teamwork!

Depend on each other when the tasting room gets super-busy
or when you're feeling a little frazzled. When you can't seem
to satisfy a customer or when you don't know the answer to a
question, it's time to call in one of your associates. That might
be your manager, or someone on the staff who is an expert on
a particular varietal or perhaps on production or some other
element of winemaking.

Calling in one of your team shows that your guest's concerns
are important to you. Introduce your "expert" by his or her
title, rephrase the question or the issue, and add something
like, *"I know that Suzanne will be able to explain this to you."*

On those crowded weekend days at Clos du Val in the Napa
Valley, when everyone is scrambling to keep up with the

welcomes and the wine pours and the personal attention to visitors, Tasting Room Associate Bill Adrian comes up with ways to lighten the mood and give staff behind the counter a break. He suggests, *"When you walk by a group of guests, say something like this."*

> *"Wow, you must be celebrating a special occasion with that reserve Cabernet (or that bubbly)."*
>
> *"How are you liking that dry Riesling?"*
>
> *"How about a special pour of one of our library wines?"*

Speaking at Special Events

When you are holding forth in front of the entire room of seated wine tasters, you have the opportunity to expand on the fascinating winery history and stories that management loves for you to tell. And as you engage with your rapt audience of guests there to enjoy themselves, you can add benefits to your facts about the wine, and really be engaging by asking questions of the group.

The challenge may be to draw them out and get them to respond, or it may be to get them to stop talking so you can do your job.

A great idea from Claire, a host at Cakebread Cellars, is to have guests introduce themselves and say what they do, or did, for a living, and/or what brings them to the valley or to your winery. By drawing out each guest, she finds that you connect with them in a personal way, and later, they may begin to bond with each other. Think of ways to involve the group, such as conducting a wine contest at the end of the tasting, with each person voting for the wine they would award as the winner. This could very smoothly lend itself to closing sales: "Can we package up your winners to take home?"

Separate Tables

At seated tastings when you are pouring wine at many tables, your time with each person is limited. Such wineries as Gloria Ferrer have a knack for connecting with each guest in a charming way. They linger at each table, asking questions and getting conversations started.

As you pour, try to get the attention of each table and describe each wine, taking care to add a benefit to every fact, all the while coming across as your charming self!

When a lot of people are scattered at tables around the room, the quick, direct close works best:

"Which ones may I package up for you?"

"Would you like to take some home?"

"How about remembering this beautiful evening by taking home some of this fabulous wine?"

"Which was your favorite tonight?"

"Have you made your choices?

If you have encouraged them to take notes throughout the tasting, ask to see the notes and make a few comments ("I see you zeroed in on the Zinfandel. How about taking some home tonight?") Close on the ones they checked off on the menu.

Winemaker Dinners

They came to eat, socialize, drink wine and have fun (and most likely paid a substantial price to do it). While they may be interested in what you have to say, they will be noisy, talking while you are talking, and even ignoring you. I suggest keeping your remarks to a minimum and deliberately adding enticing benefits to your facts about the wine, and using lots of romance words. After your main presentation, visit each table and be friendly, upbeat and charming. You are the winery, and you may be the entertainment. This is the time to boost your "like factor."

YOUR THOUGHTS

Describe three things that are unique about your winery and the tasting experience that you offer:

_____

_____

_____

_____

_____

_____

Describe a unique and effective way in which you deal with a big group.

_____

_____

_____

_____

_____

_____

_____

_____

_____

_____

_____

EIGHT   Your Worst Day: Handling Crises

An unhappy customer is no problem when you know what to say and do. First, find out about your management's policies for dealing with difficult customers, and discuss various scenarios that might come up.

You cannot control anyone else's behavior; you can only control your own responses. Always remain courteous and non-reactive. . . stay cool and calm. Never argue or tell someone they are wrong. Be gracious, no matter what!

Relax and Listen

Keeping in mind that 85% of our communication is non-verbal, use open facial and body language. Don't cross your arms and frown. Keep your eyebrows up, and avoid saying, *"You'll have to . . .,"* which are words that provoke most people.

As if you've never heard the complaint before, listen attentively and do not interrupt. Call them by name, respectfully ("Susan, let's see if we can work this out for you.") Apologize for any inconvenience and avoid giving excuses or defending yourself or the winery. Think of yourself as a 911 operator: get the facts straight, promise a solution, and calm the customer. Use "us" and "we" instead of "you," and say things such as,

> I'm sure we can make this right.
>
> Why don't I arrange for . . .
>
> I'll check and get right back to you.
>
> I know we can solve this.

Your bottom line is to maintain a good relationship with each and every visitor (no matter how crabby!), and to come across as friendly and accommodating to anyone who may be watching and listening. This is when you turn a negative situation into an opportunity to render creative customer service and get a lifelong, faithful customer.

A winery host that I know walked up to a guest in the gift shop and said to her, "May I show you that item?" to which she replied, "Would you just get out of my face!" His friendliness meter running on high, he said, "I know just how you feel. I hate to be hounded when I'm shopping, too. Please take your time and browse as long as you like."
What a pro!

Tough Questions and Objections

In my winery hospitality workshops, I ask the attendees to describe to me their least favorite questions, complaints and comments from their winery visitors, then, I have everyone practice answers that satisfy both themselves and their guests. Preparing in advance a calm, unrushed, well-thought-out answer takes the awkwardness out of it for everyone involved.

Some common questions and objections that tasting room staffers get:

> Why is your wine so expensive?
>
> Do you ever have qualms about selling alcohol?
>
> I better not join the club today. . .buy wine today. . .because. . .
>
> We already have too much at home.
>
> I'm not sure.
>
> I don't want to pay the shipping.
>
> We already own too much wine.
>
> We belong to too many wine clubs.
>
> Your wine is too expensive.
>
> We live too far away to come to your events.

In some cases, resistance by your guests is just a natural or even a habitual reaction when in a retail atmosphere. When approached in a store, after being greeted, customers often say, "No thank you, just looking." And then they might say, "Do you have this in red?" In fact, they are there to buy, but their first response is rejection!

To answer their rejections with a scripted response just pushes them away psychologically. No one likes a hard-sell—and I know that's not your style. My recommendation is to walk in their shoes. Show understanding of their feelings by saying:

> Many people feel as you do.
>
> I can see why you say that.
>
> I hear that a lot these days.
>
> I understand.
>
> I agree with you.

"We have just started to visit wineries. Maybe later."

Express your understanding of their feelings, then as the tasting proceeds, encourage them to make notes on the tasting menu. At the end of the tasting if they still are not ready to buy, give them your card, or write your name and phone number on the menu, and tell them to feel free to call you at the end of the day. Offer to have their wine choices all ready for them to pick up; and, your winery may also offer delivery to their hotel.

"Your wine is just too expensive."

Keep it conversational and non-confrontive by using lighthearted responses such as "I know exactly how you feel!" Take away the perceived negative about the price and by changing it to a powerful reason for purchasing that pricey wine. You can say, "I certainly do see where you are coming from. These are considered the best Cabernets made in this region and they are limited in production. You might want to consider them for that very special occasion you mentioned, and for when you want to bring back the memory of your visit!"

"We already belong to too many wine clubs"

Try saying something like, "I know what you mean. A lot of avid wine lovers find themselves in several wine clubs before they know it! One solution is to rotate your club memberships, dropping out of an old one when you join a new one."

Your courtesy, your attention to their objections, and your absence of pushiness all go a long way. It is your intention and your attitude that are remembered, not your selling tactics. You not only sold wine, you started a relationship. Who do you think they will recommend to their friends?

I've heard that some visitors call, after arriving home, to arrange for wine shipment and to express thanks to their host!

Grumbles and Complaints

Consider yourself a consultant who solves problems. You already know what people are likely to ask you and what they complain about, if they do complain. So, put on your consultant's hat, rephrase or reiterate the comment or the question to show that you are taking it seriously, then give your best information or advice. Consultive selling is empathy backed by product knowledge.

Remember you are selling, serving and educating. Never treat an objection or a complaint with contempt, no matter how silly or unreasonable it may seem. Use cushioning words like these:

I understand that you could be concerned about . . .

I can see how you might think that.

In answer to your concerns about serving alcohol, we take great pride in promoting our wines as enhancements to food, and we always recommend moderate drinking.

You know, I often get that question.

I see your point of view.

I know exactly what you mean.

Thank you for letting us know.

If you have no good answer to a complaint, just say, *"I never thought about it that way before."* Or, offer to find out more and give the customer a call later. Sometimes, people just want to hear themselves complain and they don't expect or need an answer or a solution. Assume a warm, open look and allow him or her to sound off until they have said it all (so they can save face).

Be gracious, apologize for any inconvenience, and when there is nothing else you can do, ask for their name and contact information, and promise to follow up (giving you a chance to talk to management). Then, just smile!

YOUR THOUGHTS

Describe your worst day. What did you do? How did it end?

_____

_____

_____

_____

What did you learn from that experience?

_____

_____

_____

_____

_____

_____

NINE   Wine Club Sign-Ups

Wine clubs are high profit centers for your winery, and depending on your financial arrangement with your employer, profitable for you, too. And, they are by far the most effective method for maintaining a long-term relationship with customers.

Welcome to the Family

Wine club members are made to feel like part of the family when winery owners, winemakers and staff get to know them and greet them like old friends at the various club events throughout the year. It's great fun for wine lovers to be "insiders" who get a look at the Great and Powerful Oz behind the curtain!

> *At the small, farmlike Tres Sabores winery in the Napa Valley, members of the "Wine Society of Tres Sabores" are treated like close friends. I watched the owner/winemaker, Julie Johnson, greet a group of club members as they arrived to pick up their allotments. She stopped what she was doing and came out to hug them and chat about news of the wine year.*

Spin tales of club events that you've attended, and make them sound irresistible. I recall stories of how a winery owner played the saxophone with the jazz band, and how a Wild West party involved everyone wearing cowboy boots and hats. Some wine clubs offer wine-themed cruises, and farm-to-table feasts right in the vineyards.

Questions and concerns you may get from guests who are considering the wine club:

> Can I choose what wines I want in the (monthly, semi-annual) shipment?
>
> Do wine club members get additional case discounts?
>
> Can I bring guests to the club events?
>
> We already belong to three other wine clubs.
>
> I'm not sure we'll be back here to go to the member events.

Making membership available is one of the nicest things you could do for your visitors. By letting them know about the benefits of your wine club, you are doing them a favor.

**Don't just hand a wine club brochure to your guests.
Offer a special invitation to join your winery family!**

Make this a personal invitation that will make your guests feel important, cared about, and included in an exclusive group. Always make the offer, saying, *"I invite you to join our family of wine lovers! You are a perfect fit."*

If all else fails and your guest(s) decide not to sign up for the club, ask for their contact information anyway, so that you can follow up with an email or a postcard. Offer your business card, so they can call you later for questions and for shipping. (On your card, use a title such as Wine Educator, Brand Ambassador, or Wine Consultant; and never use the title "Server.")

Wine club members may make private appointments for wine tasting. Before they arrive, be sure to research their wine-buying history. Your club members will love it when you already know what they like, and especially when you offer a chance for them to purchase the last few bottles of a particular vintage that is not available to the general public.

Member Retention

One of the main concerns now at many wineries is the tendency for people to cancel their club memberships.

Keeping members in the winery family is much like how we keep our personal relationships healthy and growing. Pay attention to them! Treat them like they are special and important. Wine club managers, and often hospitality hosts and other winery employees, keep their member relationships alive and well with ongoing contact through emails, phone conversations, direct mail, and invitations.

When visiting with Ellen Reich Luchtel, co-founder of Fortunati Vineyards and Winery, I learned some ways to keep wine club relationships alive and well. Besides all their electronic and phone communications, they include a gift with every club shipment, such as lovely decanters and wine accessories. Some of the gifts are one-in-a-kind, creating a lasting impression, and the thank-you cards are hand-written! The high-end members get extra-special gifts such as large-format, dummy bottles with etched logos. for display in wine cellars. Ellen told me that this personal touch has been well worth it, making her members feel like they are her number one priority.

St. Francis Winery in the Sonoma Valley sent me a "We miss you" email offering 30% off on my next shipment if I agreed to return to the club! Discounts can work, especially if they are in hand-written notes or a personal phone call. Also, Tablas Creek Vineyard in Paso Robles sends their members very nice, unique Christmas gifts.

The club manager at Francis Ford Coppola Winery made a personal phone call to me, saying, "You can't be leaving us!" They also send gifts with every shipment.

When you invite people into your wine club "family," treat them like family! Stay in touch. Give them a call, a gift, and a sense of importance. When they come into your winery, treat them like the very special people they are. Remember, it's showtime! You're on.

YOUR THOUGHTS

Describe several ways in which you can improve your
club membership sales.

_____

_____

_____

_____

Which wine club members have you contacted recently?

_____

_____

_____

_____

TEN Follow-Up, Come Back Soon!

Reinforcing the Sale

Your job isn't over yet. After a purchase has been made, affirm the sale and make your guests feel great about it by saying:

> You're going to love this.
>
> This is going to be so perfect for your party.
>
> You picked my two personal favorites.
>
> After you've opened this at home, go to our Facebook page and let us know how you liked it!
> We'd love to know.
>
> I know it will remind you of this day in the valley.
>
> If you'd like to leave me your contact information, I can let you know of special sales and events.

Affirm your guest's buying choice every time they buy, and congratulate them as new club members.

Let your customer know that you are always happy to hear from them, and that the winery values their relationship and their business.

Make a production of a purchase by walking out from behind your counter and presenting it to your guest. Here's a tip from Nordstrom's, a retail chain famous for brand loyalty and customer service: *"Salespeople are taught to walk the bagged purchase around the counter to the customer, rather than just handing it across the counter."*

Leave your guests on a high note by saying, "Do keep your wine list so that when you get home, you can remember the ones you liked the best. And, don't hesitate to call me and I'll have it shipped right out!

> *When people have a good experience at your winery they will tell up to 5 people. When they have negative experiences, they will tell 15 or more people.*

Good-bye and Thank You

Taking the time to send an email or a note to your guests can pay off. You'll be surprised by how impressed, even touched, people can be when, after they arrive home, they receive a nice note of thanks. I treasure the personal notes I received from the hosts at Brooks Wine in Oregon and Castoro Cellars in Paso Robles. The most successful and well-liked winery sales professionals cultivate the customer connection and ensure future sales with phone calls, emails and notes in the mail; and, those are the customers who are most apt to tell their friends about their special treatment. (Not everyone will want to share their contact information and you don't want to alienate them. Try just asking for a business card!)

I know that you go the extra mile for your guests and for your winery every day, and on some days, it may hard to come up with that sprinkle of pixie dust that makes every guest experience just perfect. So, I hope my advice and techniques will help you get more enjoyment and satisfaction out of representing your winery. When you have waved your magic wand and created once-in-a-lifetime experiences for your visitors, every time they see your label on a wine list and every time they return to your corner of the world, your winery will be on their minds. Thanks to you, they will always think of your winery as "their" winery.

YOUR THOUGHTS

After your guests depart the tasting room, ask yourself, "What did I learn about them?"

Where are they from? _____

How did they find us? _____

Did I get their contact information? _____

What were their favorite wines? _____

_____

What details about them did I learn: work, family, personality, other?

_____

_____

_____

_____

_____

SAVIGNON BLANC

From Lynda

This book isn't going to immediately change how you present and sell wine at your tasting room or at winery events. For lasting results and huge success as a brand ambassador and hospitality host, make notes here in the handbook on the best ideas, tips and suggestions you got from *Romancing the Grape*, then transfer each of them to a 3X5 card.

With these cards as your guides, practice your newly acquired presentation skills, vocabulary, and friendly, welcoming demeanor!

If you are willing to take the time to absorb and take ownership of the selling and relationship fundamentals in this book, you will see significant benefits. Your selling skills will improve greatly, as will your confidence, and your enjoyment of dealing with people in all areas of your life.

Make *Romancing the Grape* work for you and have fun with it. Remember, establishing a new habit (or breaking an old one) takes at least twenty-one days. *Let me know how it goes! I'd love to hear from you.*

My very best,
Lynda Paulson

775-530-6119
Lynda@SuccessStrategiesInc.com
SuccessStrategiesInc.com

A special message for the trainer or the person responsible for the success of the hospitality staff selling the wine!

No matter how productive a motivational workshop or this book may be, the benefits to your hospitality associates fade in time. Rather than a one-time event, wine sales training must be an on-going process.

At Success Strategies, Inc., we offer a "Train the Trainer" session following every one of our **Winery Hospitality and Relationship Sales Training** workshops. No exception. No extra fee.

You can use *Romancing the Grape* to complement your own in-house training. I suggest following this format:

- Cover one selling fundamental at a time

- After each chapter, have them write down when they would use the sales fundamental, how they would say it, and to whom.

- Ask them to say their sales prompts to you and to a partner. (The more they internalize their new words and phrases, the more they will own them and use them.)

- Use 3x5 flash cards, too! It is amazing how effective they can be.

In a group or one-on-one, your wine sales training can be done at the beginning of the day before your visitors arrive, when your interactive presentation will be fresh in their minds. Expect major payoffs!

Your praise and encouragement go a long way. Be sure to let your brand ambassadors and tasting room hosts know how important they are to the success of the winery. Remind them that to their tasting room guests, they ARE the winery.

Call me for some fun team games and coaching ideas!

Purchase *Romancing the Grape* from:
SuccessStrategiesInc.com.
For individual and bulk purchases of the book, and special
pricing, just give me a call!

—All the best, Lynda
775-530-6119
SuccessStrategiesInc.com

About the Author

Lynda R. Paulson has received widespread recognition as a communication skills and public speaking coach for more than 35 years. Her coaching techniques have been crafted over decades for clientele such as AT&T, American Express, Disney Corporation, Getty Fuel. She has also worked with more than 600 wineries in California, Oregon, Washington, New York, and Canada.

Paulson's popular in-house and public **Winery Hospitality & Relationship Sales** Training workshops are legendary throughout the wine world. Highly participatory, the workshops involve discovery of communication strengths, building poise and confidence, and above all, developing relationship sales expertise.

The author of *Success Strategies for Retail Selling*, and *The Executive Persuader: How to Be a Powerful Speaker*, she has published many articles on sales, customer service, people management, and team building, and is on the Board of Directors of Wine Women.

She is also renowned across the United States for founding and leading the **Executive Speaking Experience,** a powerful, personal, interactive program focused on public speaking and presentation skills for very small groups of individuals; and, she has coached numerous business executives, celebrities, wine critics, and thought leaders to prepare and present their messages. Formerly a Vice-President at Dale Carnegie Training, she was also their first woman instructor in the United States.

Paulson lives in Incline Village, Nevada, with her husband, and her black lab, Cabernet.

www.SuccessStrategiesInc.com

CABERNET SAUVIGNON

www.ingramcontent.com/pod-product-compliance
Lightning Source LLC
Chambersburg PA
CBHW081550220326
41598CB00036B/6626